Hello dear reader

Welcome to the wonderful and magical
world of the Disney Princesses. Join us in creating
the amazing hairstyles of Ariel, Belle, Aurora, Rapunzel,
Mulan, Pocahontas, Merida, Tiana, Cinderella, Snow White
and Jasmine. In this book you will find hairstyles for all the
princesses with step by step photographs and instructions.
We encourage you to try as many hairstyles as you can and
use them as inspiration to create your own look, you can
even mix some of the styles together to create a new one.
We hope you enjoy taking this adventure with us!

Have fun!

Ariel's Locks

1. Take hold of a fairly large lock of hair at the front on one side.
2. Braid down the lock (see the Braidschool, p. 8).
3. Hold one part of the braid in one hand and the other two in the other hand.
4. Slide the two parts together up the lock.
5. Don't be afraid to slide it high up.
6. Pull the parts back down a little way and tie off the end with an elastic band.
7. Fix the locks of hair to even out the gaps between the twists.
8. Repeat the whole process on the other side of the head and join the finished locks in an elastic band at the back of the head.

Aurora's Forest

1. Make a side part in the front. Comb the hair on both sides of the face over it. Put a hairband over the hair in front of the ears.
2. Take the hair in front of the ears on one side and twist it.
3. When the lock of hair has been thoroughly twisted, hold one end with one hand and pull the twist with the other hand to increase its volume and shape.
4. It works well to let the child hold the twist while making a similar twist on the other side of the head.
5. Join the two twists at the back of the head.
6. Tie them with an elastic band.
7. Twist the hair from the small ponytail at the back below the secured twists and form a rose around the elastic band.
8. Pin the rose down by hooking a bobby pin into the rose and the hair underneath and press in.

Belle's Bow

1. Take two locks of hair from both sides in the front and twist them.
2. Join the two locks in the back with a small elastic band.
3. Put another elastic band around the ponytail and form a loop by pulling half the lock down from the elastic band.
4. Divide the loop in two and bring the hair from the ponytail over the twist that you made first.
5. Bring the hair from the ponytail once around the middle of the loop that you made and back behind the twist.
6. Pin the ponytail completely down next to the knot that has formed.
7. Now fix the bow by pulling its loops to opposite sides.

Cinderella's Bun

1. Divide the hair in two parts, horizontally across the back of the head.
2. Put the lower part in a high ponytail.
3. Place a hair doughnut around the ponytail and lightly pin it to the hair underneath. Divide the ponytail in two.
4. Wrap one part around the doughnut.
5. Pin it down. It works well to hook the hair and doughnut in the hair underneath to fasten the bun securely.
6. Now wrap the other part of the ponytail around the doughnut in the opposite direction from before.
7. Pin the hair down securely
8. Put a pretty hairband over the hair at the front.
9. Take the hair from one side and bring it to the back and up along the bun.
10. Fasten the ends of the hair up against the bun and take the hair from the other side.
11. Repeat the process from before.
12. Fix the hair, pin it down and spray at will.

Jasmine's Ponytail

1. Take fairly large locks of hair from both sides of the head and twist them.
2. Join the twists at the back of the head and tie them with an elastic band.
3. Pull the twists out at will.
4. Tie the hair with an elastic band half-way down the length.
5. Pull the hair out at the sides.
6. Tie another elastic band at the bottom and pull the hair in between out at the sides.

Merida's Curls

1. Make a center part from the forehead to the back of the head. A pintail comb works well for a clean parting.
2. Use the end of the comb to create a line from the end of the middle parting approximately to the cheekbone.
3. Put an elastic band around this section.
4. Repeat on the other side of the middle parting.
5. Stick the end of a topsy tail™ down into one ponytail, above the elastic band.
6. Put the hair from the ponytail through the topsy tail™.
7. Pull the topsy tail™ with the hair through.
8. Tighten the ponytail.
9. Do the same thing on the other side.

Mulan's Twists and Turns

1. Make a box like division in the hair on the top of the head and fasten the rest of the hair with a clip.
2. Take a lock of hair along the hairline and make a horizontal division and put the rest of the big lock in a clip.
3. Put a small elastic band in the small lock by the end of the box like division.
4. Take another lock just behind the first one and put an elastic band in it as before.
5. Repeat the process along the top of the hair until all the lock has been put into elastic bands.
6. Take a topsy tail™ and put it under the elastic band.
7. Put the hair from the small lock and put it into the hole in the topsy tail™.
8.-9. Pull the topsy tail™ all the way through the ponytail.
10. Make the ponytail a bit firmer.
11. Repeat the process along the top of the hair

Pocahontas's Hidden Braid

1. Divide the hair in two parts, horizontally across the back of the head. Gather the lower part in a ponytail.
2. Make a French braid (see the Braidschool, p. 9) with the upper part. Start at the front by the forehead.
3. Braid all the way down the length.
4. Fasten with an elastic band at the end.
5. Undo the ponytail in the lower section and divide in two.
6. Criss-cross the two parts over the braid, under it, and over again.
7. Join the braid and the two parts with an elastic band at the end.

Rapunzel's Full Braid

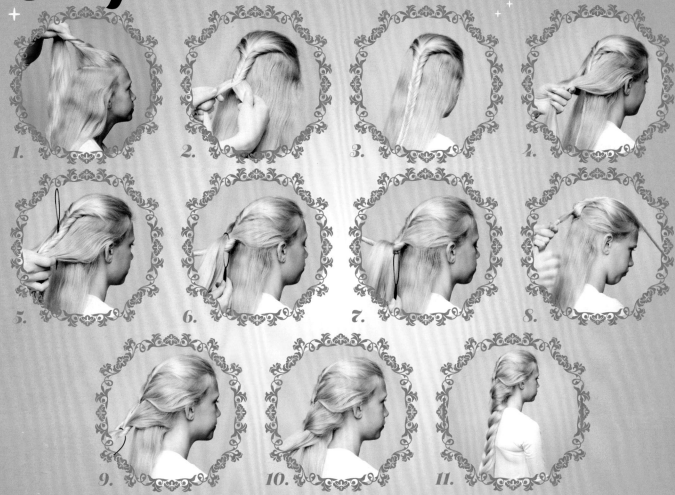

1. Make a "horseshoe" part and take hold of the hair on top.
2. In that section make a fishtail braid all the way down the length (see the Braidschool, p. 12).
3. Tie the end with an elastic band.
4. Take hold of two large locks of hair from either side of the head.
5. Stick a topsy tail™ high in the fishtail.
6. Put the locks from the sides through the eye of the topsy tail™.
7. Pull the topsy tail™ with the locks through the fishtail.
8. Lift the fishtail away and join the locks with a small elastic band.
9. Take another two locks, in similar size to earlier locks, below the first locks. Stick the topsy tail™ into the fishtail. Pull it through with the locks as before. Try to keep the gap between the locks equal in length.
10. Continue with this method down the fishtail braid.
11. When you have reached all the way down, put an elastic band at the end.

Snow White Ribbon

1. 2. 3. 4.

5. 6. 7. 8.

9. 10.

1. Take hold of a small lock of hair, close to the face in the middle. Fasten a long ribbon to the lock with an elastic band.
2. Now make a side part in the hair and put the hair over the ribbon. Take hold of a lock by the part with one hand and hold the ribbon with the other.
3. Wrap the lock once around the ribbon. The lock now appears closer to the face and the ribbon away from the face.
4. Add hair to the lock and wrap it once around the ribbon.
5. Repeat the process, taking care of how the hair falls into the twist.
6. Wrap the lock around the ribbon each time hair is added.
7. Continue this method down along the hairline.
8. When all the hair has been added to the twist, tie the hair and the ribbon with an elastic band close to the roots.
9. Fold the ribbon and tie it around the elastic band.
10. Tie the ribbon into a bow.

Tiana's Braid

1. Gather the hair from closest to the forehead to the back of the head.
2. Pin the hair down by hooking a bobby pin into the locks and pushing it into the hair in the opposite direction. This way the pin is secured and cannot be seen.
3. Roughly gather the hair from the side that was left behind and criss-cross the locks one over the other below what you first did.
4. Carefully pin the hair using the same method as before.
5. Take another two similar locks from each side and move to the back of the head.
6. Pin the locks together, using the same method as before.
7. Repeat the process down the length, or until all the hair has been gathered in the hairstyle.
8. Tuck the ends in towards the nape of the neck if necessary and pin down.

Disney Princess Hairstyles

-11 Beautiful Princess Hairstyles With Step by Step Images

Author: Theodora Mjoll Skuladottir Jack
Photographer: Gassi.is
Set designer and stylist: Ellen Lofts
Layout and design: Bjarney Hinriksdottir
Cover design: Gassi.is
Editors: Tinna Proppe, tinna@eddausa.com
Printed in Canada
Distributed by Midpoint Book Sales & Distribution

ISBN 978-1-94078-706-0
www.eddausa.com